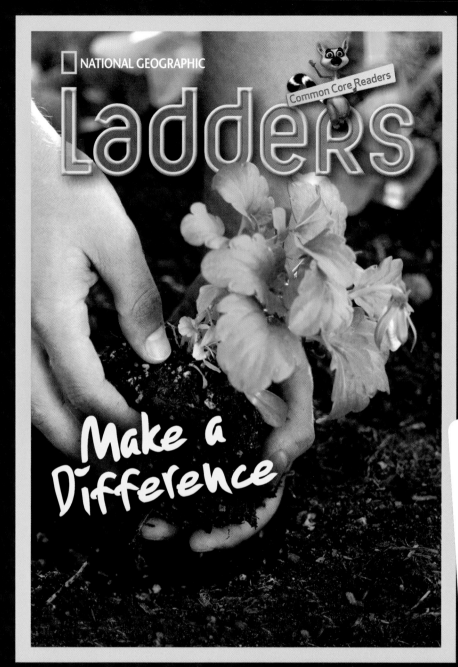

NATIONAL GEOGRAPHIC

Common Core Readers

Ladders

Make a
Difference

T0308484

Jane Addams: Champion of the Poor 2
    by Jennifer A. Smith

Stone Soup 10
    retold by Michael Murphy
    illustrated by Colin Jack

Community Gardens Make a Difference . . 20
    by Jennifer A. Smith

Discuss 24

Jane Addams
Champion of the Poor
by Jennifer A. Smith

What does it mean to "make a difference"? It means making the world a better place through your actions and words. The **impact,** or difference you make, can be big or small—it doesn't matter. What's important is the good you do!

Jane Addams speaking to a group of children at Hull House

Jane Addams was one person who made a big difference. Addams was one of the most important social **reformers** in American history. Through her efforts, she helped improve the well-being of thousands of poor families so they could live healthier, happier lives.

Jane was born in 1860 in Cedarville, Illinois. Her father, John Huy Addams, was an Illinois state senator and a friend of Abraham Lincoln. Mr. Addams helped teach Jane the importance of social **justice,** or fairness for all. Jane's hunger for social justice would lead her to found Hull House, one of the first settlement houses in North America.

Toynbee Hall began in London in 1884. It was the world's first settlement house. Visiting Toynbee Hall inspired Addams and Ellen Gates Starr. They wanted to try the idea in Chicago.

What is a settlement house? It's a social support organization that helps people in poor communities get better jobs and more education. Often these people are immigrants—people from other countries who have come to the United States to live. Settlement houses first got their name because social workers settled, or moved into, poor immigrant neighborhoods. A social worker is a person who is trained to help others improve their lives. Social workers thought living in the poorest communities was important to helping community members seek better **opportunities.**

Hull House was named after its builder Charles Hull.

Addams and her friend Ellen Gates Starr were inspired by a settlement house they visited during a trip to London. They decided they would try the idea back home in America.

After returning from Europe, Addams and Starr raised money for a settlement house. Eventually they rented property in a working-class, immigrant neighborhood in Chicago, Illinois. In 1889 they moved in and opened the doors to Hull House.

Hull House began as just one building. It later grew to include 13 buildings, a playground, and a camp in Wisconsin. The buildings eventually took up half a city block. They included an art gallery and a gymnasium. Donations of money and property contributed to its growth. Within two years, Hull House was assisting as many as 2,000 people every week!

As a settlement house, the goal was to help people help themselves. The many opportunities Hull House offered reflected its aim of improving lives in every way. Neighborhood residents could participate in college-level courses, art classes, and a theater group. They could also get trained in various jobs. Community members had use of a day care center, a kitchen, and a library.

Addams and other reformers at Hull House also worked on larger social issues, such as getting rid of **sweatshops.** During this time period, many immigrants worked in factories known as sweatshops. In sweatshops, workers would put in long hours for little pay. The conditions were often filthy and dangerous. Even some children had to work so they could earn money for their families instead of going to school. Eventually an Illinois law was passed in 1893. The law banned children under the age of 14 from working in sweatshops. It also required sweatshops to follow better safety standards.

Girls and boys could take dancing lessons at Hull House.

Boys worked all night at this glass-making factory.

A summer art class at Hull House

This banner advertises an upcoming speech by Addams in 1913. Women in the United States did not gain the right to vote until 1920.

Jane Addams's impact as a reformer and defender of justice could be felt in other areas, too. Addams believed in and fought for women's right to vote. In 1915 she organized women to protest World War I. As a result of her efforts, Addams received the Nobel Peace Prize in 1931. She was the first American woman ever to receive this famous award.

Helping others was the guiding force of Jane Addams's influential life. She understood that, when given the opportunity, people could succeed in many ways. Her impact as a founder of Hull House and supporter of workers, women, and peace lives on to this day. The world could always use more people like Jane Addams!

The Jane Addams Hull
House Museum in Chicago

In 2012 the Jane Addams Hull House Association announced it
was closing after 122 years. It was a sad day. The association
was helping more than 60,000 people each year, but there wasn't
enough money to carry on the effort. Thankfully hundreds of other
settlement houses continue to make a difference every day in
neighborhoods across the United States.

Check In   Why did Addams and Starr open Hull House?

Stone Soup

retold by Michael Murphy
illustrated by Colin Jack

Mr. Fox, a hungry traveler, decided he would seek his next meal in a nearby village. On his way there, some fellow travelers warned him it would be no use. "Don't even bother," they said, "for these villagers are very poor and, to make matters worse, they **quarrel.** The neighbors accuse one other of stealing food. They do not share among themselves, let alone with strangers. No, indeed, you will have no luck there, my friend."

Where others saw a hopeless situation, Mr. Fox saw an **opportunity,** for he was a sly and clever old fox. He searched the woods till he found what he was looking for: a smooth and round stone of just the right size for a pot. Mr. Fox cleaned and polished the stone with the sleeve of his shirt. Then he put it in his pocket and headed into the village.

Good luck was with Mr. Fox. The first house he approached belonged to Mrs. Squirrel, who was tending the potatoes in her garden. As she was quite nosey, she could not resist finding out what the stranger wanted.

"Simply the loan of a cooking pot, Madam," said the fox politely. "Then I could rest in the **commons** and make stone soup for my supper."

His words made quite an **impact** on the curious squirrel. She was dying to know what stone soup was. And if she lent the stranger her cooking pot, she would have an opportunity to eat something other than nuts and potatoes.

In the commons—the public space in the center of this village—Mr. Fox lit a cooking fire. He filled the squirrel's pot with water and dropped the stone into the pot, stirring it with a wooden spoon. Mrs. Squirrel looked on from her doorway. After a time, Mr. Fox raised the spoon to his mouth and took a sip.

"Ah, yes, it's very good," he said to Mrs. Squirrel. "I would offer you some, but this is not the proper way to have stone soup. It needs potatoes to bring out the rich flavor of the stone. But, alas, I have none."

"I have potatoes!" said Mrs. Squirrel, who was eager to try the stone soup.

Mr. Fox managed to look pleasantly surprised when she hurried back with an armful of big, tasty-looking potatoes.

The shy Miss Rabbit
had been watching all of
this with a great deal of interest. Reluctantly
she decided to investigate what the commotion was about.
After all, it was making her jumpy.

Quietly she crept into the commons and sniffed the air. She imagined
how nice it would be to eat something other than carrots for a change.

"Stone soup," said the fox kindly, so the rabbit wouldn't have to
ask. "It would smell wonderful. But, alas, it lacks the aroma of carrots,
because I have none. Stone soup is just not at its best without carrots."

"I suppose I do have some carrots," offered Miss Rabbit nervously.

Mr. Fox managed to look both astonished and overjoyed when she
hurried back to the commons clutching several large carrots.

Prickly Mr. Porcupine had been watching all of this with growing suspicion. It made him quite cross, not being invited! The porcupine marched over to where the others were watching the pot, intending to take charge of the situation.

"Here you are!" cried Mr. Fox warmly. "As I'm sure you already know, we're making stone soup. You must have had it many times."

Mr. Porcupine had no earthly idea what stone soup was. Of course nothing would make him admit this.

"Unfortunately," continued Mr. Fox, "I would be embarrassed to offer you any because, alas, I don't have any peas. I'm sure you've *never* eaten stone soup without peas before!"

Mr. Porcupine said, somewhat gruffly, "I have peas."

With his sharp eyes, Mr. Fox had practically *counted* the peas in the porcupine's garden already. Still, he managed to look both astounded and thrilled when Mr. Porcupine hurried back to the commons with dozens of plump little peas.

And so it was that Mr. Porcupine, Miss Rabbit, Mrs. Squirrel, Mr. Fox, and a few curious neighbors all sat down to eat together. What a fine opportunity to mend quarrels.

At last Mr. Fox said he must be on his way. He thanked the villagers for the opportunity to dine with them.

"Don't forget your wonderful stone," the villagers said together.

But Mr. Fox said he knew where to get another one, and this stone was his gift to them. "I only ask that you share it with one another and with hungry strangers."

And, of course, they promised they would.

Later that evening, Mr. Fox again saw his fellow travelers. He told them he had gone to the village in spite of their warnings.

They laughed and said, "Did you have any luck?"

"Indeed I did," replied Mr. Fox. "Potluck."

MORAL *People are better off when they share with one another.*

Check In   Why did Mr. Fox leave the stone with the villagers?

Community Gardens Make a Difference

by Jennifer A. Smith

What is a community garden? Unlike the private gardens people have in their yards, a community garden is a group of several smaller gardens. Each small garden is a plot of land available for free or to rent. The plots in a community garden are close together, so gardeners often get to know one another. Community gardens exist in big cities and in small towns.

Community members work together in a garden.

The benefits of joining a community garden can have a positive **impact** on you and your environment. For example, a community garden will connect you with the land and the food you eat. If the garden is in your neighborhood, it will strengthen your community since you will get to know more of your neighbors. A community garden will offer you healthier food options, too.

Community gardeners can sell what they grow at a food stand. Gardens can help people earn money!

Ask any community gardener to describe what he or she likes about it. Most will include something about the satisfaction they get from **investing** their time and energy in the land. Often, a gardener's satisfaction, or enjoyment, grows right along with the garden itself. You, too, can experience this sense of fulfillment.

Community gardens have social benefits. They improve society by providing a natural meeting place for neighborhood residents to visit with one another. Growers can trade gardening secrets or just talk about the weather. Therefore, community gardens help build friendships and strengthen community ties.

Joining a community garden will give you the **opportunity** to grow your own **produce,** such as fruits and vegetables, which can make you healthier. How? A wide variety of produce is an important part of a healthy diet. Garden food is also fresher than grocery store food; therefore, it's more nutritious *and* tastier.

Community gardens provide many benefits to their members. These include personal enjoyment, an opportunity for socializing, and a healthier diet. So consider joining a community garden! By investing in a garden, you are investing in your community.

People of all ages can help tend a garden.

Discuss Main Ideas

1. What do you think connects the three pieces that you read in this book? What makes you think that?

2. How do you think Jane Addams made a difference? Cite evidence from the text to support your answer.

3. Choose the squirrel, the rabbit, or the porcupine. Describe the character. Then explain why the character is better off at the end of the story. Use evidence from the text to support your answer.

4. What is the main idea of "Community Gardens"? What are three reasons the writer gives to support the main idea?

5. What do you still wonder about any of the pieces in this book? What are some ways you could make a difference?